quilty

fresh patchwork + modern quilts

We are thrilled to bring you a collection of our very best quilts from *Quilty*! The projects in this, our first book, are some of our favorite quilts for newbies and skilled quilters alike. Whether you want to make a kid's quilt, a bed-size quilt, or one to snuggle with on the couch, we're sure you will find the perfect quilt! *Quilty* has become a magazine that quilters love. We're the go-to for the beginner who needs a teaching hand—many articles feature an online video tutorial—but readers with extensive experience come for the conversation. And everyone comes for the quilts!

Spooly and the *Quilty* Staff

SPOOLY SAYS:
"Check out
QNNtv.com/Quilty
for video tutorials!"

LEISURE ARTS®
the art of everyday living
www.leisurearts.com

Quilty
P.O. Box 171, Winterset, IA 50273
(866) 729-9601
Web site: HeyQuilty.com

Quilty Staff

Editor	Mary Fons
Managing Editor	Debra Finan
Associate Editor	Diane Tomlinson
Technical Writer	Kristine Peterson
Contributing Writers	Susan Guzman
	Nancy Mahoney
	Amy Rullkoetter
Art Director	Courtney Kraig
Contributing Photographer	Kathryn Gamble
Contributing Photo Assistant	Mary Mouw
Photo Stylist	Tony Jacobson

Operations

Publisher	Kristi Loeffelholz
Circulation Director	Deb Westmaas
New Business Manager	Lance Covert
Renewal and Billing Manager	Nekeya Dancy
Newstand Consultant	TJ Montilli
Online Subscriptions Manager	Jodi Lee
Production Manager	Dominic M. Taormina
Production Coordinator	Jennifer Creasey
Advertising Coordinator	Madalene Becker
Director Of Information Technology	Tom Judd
Retail Sales	LaRita Godfrey
Retail Manager	Sharon Hart
Web Editor	Paul Krantz
Web Specialist	Morgan Abel
Web Site Manager	Phillip Zacharias
Communication Specialist	Sheyenne Manning

New Track Media LLC

President and CEO	Stephen J. Kent
Chief Financial Officer	Mark F. Arnett
Vice President/ Group Publisher	Tina Battock
Vice President Consumer Marketing	Nicole McGuire
Vice President Production	Barbara Schmitz
Corporate Controller	Jordan Bohrer

Leisure Arts Staff

Editorial Staff

Vice President of Editorial	Susan White Sullivan
Creative Art Director	Katherine Laughlin
Publications Director	Leah Lampirez
Special Projects Director	Susan Frantz Wiles
Prepress Technician	Stephanie Johnson

Business Staff

President and Chief Executive Officer	Rick Barton
Senior Vice President of Operations	Jim Dittrich
Vice President of Finance	Fred F. Pruss
Vice President of Sales-Retail Books	Martha Adams
Vice President of Mass Market	Bob Bewighouse
Vice President of Technology and Planning	Laticia Mull Dittrich
Controller	Tiffany P. Childers
Information Technology Director	Brian Roden
Director of E-Commerce	Mark Hawkins
Manager of E-Commerce	Robert Young
Retail Customer Service Manager	Stan Raynor

Library of Congress Control Number: 2013957632
ISBN-13/EAN: 978-1-4647-1469-6
UPC: 0-28906-06265-6

Contents

Quilt Patterns

Tips & Techniques

Boot Camp

Anni

Clean lines and color blocking
make for soft minimalist heaven.

QUILT BY Heather Jones

MATERIALS

2⅛ yards pale pink

⅞ yard light pink

1⅛ yards medium pink

1⅝ yards dark pink

4¼ yards backing fabric

Twin-size quilt batting

CUTTING

Measurements include ¼" seam allowances. Border strips are exact length needed. You may want to cut them longer to allow for piecing variations.

From pale pink, cut:
- 6 (4½"-wide) lengthwise strips. From strips, cut 2 (4½" × 68½") side borders, 2 (4½" × 60½") top and bottom borders, 1 (4½" × 60½") horizontal sashing strip, and 2 (4½" × 28½") vertical sashing strips.

- 5 (2¼"-wide) lengthwise strips for binding.

From light pink, cut:
- 2 (12½"-wide) strips. From strips, cut 4 (12½") A squares.

From medium pink, cut:
- 1 (20½"-wide) strip. From strip, cut 4 (20½" × 8½") C rectangles.

- 1 (12½"-wide) strip. From strip, cut 8 (12½" × 4½") B rectangles.

From dark pink, cut:
- 1 (28½"-wide) strip. From strip, cut 4 (28½" × 8½") E rectangles.

- 1 (20½"-wide) strip. From strip, cut 8 (20½" × 4½") D rectangles.

FABRIC NOTE:
Fabrics in the quilt shown are a mix of Kona solids by Robert Kaufman and Bella fabrics by Moda.

Suitable for framing!

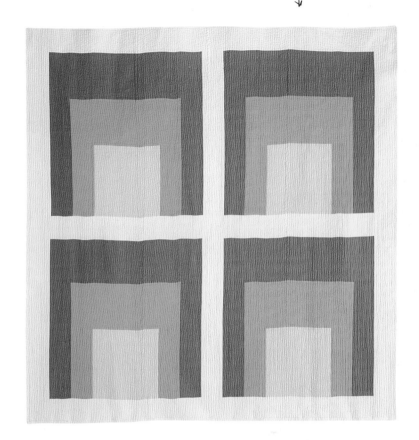

Need help sewing long seams? We walk you through it!
HeyQuilty.com/LongSeams

ENJOY THE PROCESS

Need inspiration? Go to a quilt show. Quilts are as different as the people who make them. You may find an unexpected quilt "personality" that speaks to you. Make your next quilt in that style, even if it feels foreign at first.

BLOCK ASSEMBLY

1. Lay out 1 light pink A square, 2 medium pink B rectangles, 1 medium pink C rectangle, 2 dark pink D rectangles, and 1 dark pink E rectangle as shown in Block Assembly Diagram.

2. Join in alphabetical order to complete 1 block (Block Diagram). Make 4 blocks.

3. Bask in the ease and beauty of what you just made. Boo-ya.

QUILT ASSEMBLY

1. Lay out blocks and sashing strips as shown in Quilt Top Assembly Diagram. Join into rows; join rows to complete quilt center.

2. Add pale pink top and bottom borders to quilt center. Add side borders to quilt.

FINISHING

1. Divide backing into 2 (2⅛-yard) lengths. Cut 1 piece in half lengthwise to make 2 narrow panels. Join 1 narrow panel to each side of wider panel; press seam allowances toward narrow panels.

2. Layer backing, batting, and quilt top; baste. Quilt as desired. Quilt shown was quilted with vertical lines spaced ⅜" apart (Quilting Diagram).

3. Join 2¼"-wide pale pink strips into 1 continuous piece for straight-grain French-fold binding. Add binding to quilt.

Designer Profile

Heather Jones is a designer, seamstress, and modern quilter, as well as founder and current president of the Cincinnati Modern Quilt Guild, and is working on her first line of appliqué, sewing, and quilting patterns. Three of her original quilts were chosen as winners of the Modern Quilt Guild's Project Modern Challenges, a national quilting competition. Heather and her family live in Cincinnati. For more information about Heather, visit OliveAndDollie.com.

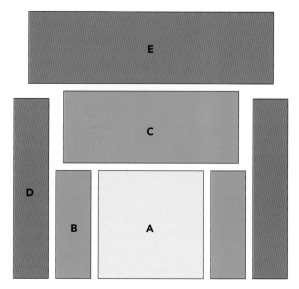

Block Assembly Diagram

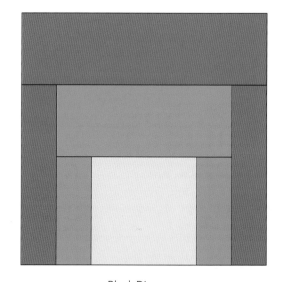

Block Diagram

BEE HAPPY

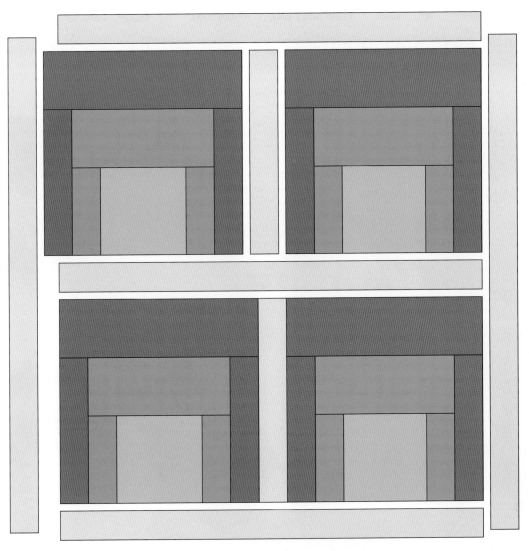

Quilt Top Assembly Diagram

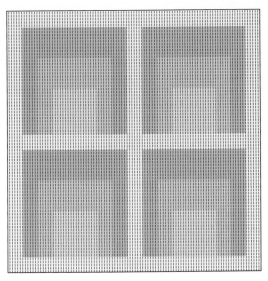

Quilting Diagram

Chevron & On

Some quilts have it all: great design, easy piecing, and style for days.

QUILT BY Megan Bohr

SPOOLY SAYS:
"This quilt was inspired by the classic houndstooth print. What classic prints or designs might you adapt?"

MATERIALS

12 fat quarters* assorted prints in orange, black, red, cream and purple for blocks

2 yards cream solid for blocks

½ yard purple stripe for binding

3½ yards backing fabric

Twin-size quilt batting

*Fat quarter = 18" × 20"

FABRIC NOTE: Fabrics in the quilt shown are Chicopee from FreeSpirit.

CUTTING

Measurements include ¼" seam allowances.

From EACH of 11 print fat quarters, cut:
- 1 (4⅞"-wide) strip. From strip, cut 4 (4⅞") squares. Cut squares in half diagonally to make 8 half-square triangles.

- 1 (4½"-wide) strip. From strip, cut 4 (4½") A squares.

From 1 print fat quarter, cut:
- 2 (4⅞"-wide) strips. From strips, cut 5 (4⅞") squares. Cut squares in half diagonally to make 10 half-square triangles.

- 1 (4½"-wide) strip. From strip (and leftover 4⅞"-wide strip), cut 5 (4½") A squares.

From cream solid, cut:
- 7 (4⅞"-wide) strips. From strips, cut 49 (4⅞") squares. Cut squares in half diagonally to make 98 half-square triangles.

- 7 (4½"-wide) strips. From strips, cut 49 (4½") A squares.

From purple stripe, cut:
- 7 (2¼"-wide) strips for binding.

BLOCK ASSEMBLY

1. Join 1 cream and 1 print half-square triangle as shown in Triangle-Square Diagrams. Make 49 pairs of matching triangle-squares.

Triangle-Square Diagrams

2. Lay out 1 pair of Triangle-Squares, 1 matching print A square, and 1 cream A square as shown in Block Assembly Diagram. Join into rows; join rows to complete 1 block (Block Diagram). Make 49 blocks.

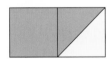

Block Assembly Diagram

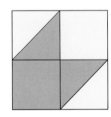

Block Diagram

QUILT ASSEMBLY

1. Lay out blocks as shown in Quilt Top Assembly Diagram on page 11.

2. Join into rows; join rows to complete quilt top.

FINISHING

1. Divide backing into 2 (1¾-yard) lengths. Cut 1 piece in half lengthwise to make 2 narrow panels. Join 1 narrow panel to wider panel; press seam allowance toward narrow panel. Remaining narrow panel is extra.

2. Layer backing, batting, and quilt top; baste. Quilt as desired. Quilt shown was quilted with pairs of straight diagonal lines (Quilting Diagram).

3. Join 2¼"-wide purple stripe strips into 1 continuous piece for straight-grain, French-fold binding. Add binding to quilt.

Designer Profile

Megan Bohr lives in rural Northeast Iowa where she designs modern quilts. Taught by her grandmother and her mother, Megan started sewing and quilting at the age of twelve and never looked back. Now, thirteen years later, she loves to share her modern sewing and quilting and inspire others on her blog, www.CanoeRidgeCreations.com.

BTW

There's a romantic notion that women on the prairie would sit by the hearth and stitch for hours by the glow of a cozy fire. Not exactly. Women on the frontier made quilts out of necessity—that they are often works of art is what makes them incredible. Women did their sewing by the window, during the day. Why? Better light.

Learn how to make other houndstooth blocks!
HeyQuilty.com/Chevron

Quilt Top Assembly Diagram

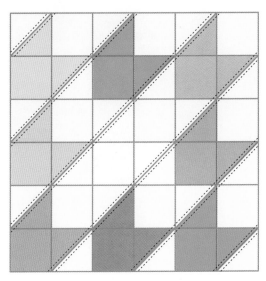

Quilting Diagram

MAKE IT YOUR OWN

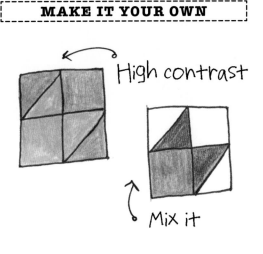

High contrast

Mix it

Kid Potential

A fun, scrappy quilt for
a kid—or the kid in you.

QUILT BY Amanda Jean Nyberg

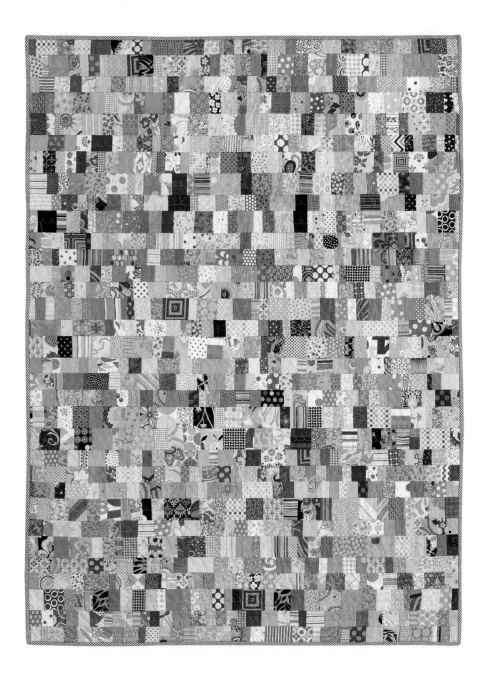

MAKE IT YOUR OWN

Sky

Stone

MATERIALS

20 fat quarters* assorted prints and solids

½ yard red check for binding

2¾ yards backing fabric

Crib-size quilt batting

*Fat quarter = 18" × 20"

CUTTING

Measurements include ¼" seam allowances.

From each fat quarter, cut:
• Strips in various widths, from 1"–3" wide.

From red check, cut:
• 224" of (2¼"-wide) bias strips. Join strips to make bias binding.

FABRIC NOTE:
Bust that stash with this great, very scrappy quilt.

STRIP SET ASSEMBLY

1. Join assorted strips randomly along long edges to make a strip set at least 15" high as shown in Strip Set Diagram. Make 11 strip sets. Go wild!

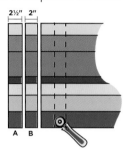

Strip Set Diagram

2. From strip sets, cut 39 (2½"-wide) A segments and 60 (2"-wide) B segments.

3. Join 3 A segments to make 1 Row 2 as shown in Row Assembly Diagram. Repeat to make 13 Row 2.

4. In the same manner, join 3 (2"-wide) B segments together to make 1 Row 1. Repeat to make 20 Row 1.

QUILT ASSEMBLY

1. Lay out rows as shown in Quilt Top Assembly Diagram. Join rows to complete quilt top.

2. Trim quilt top to measure 41½" wide.

FINISHING

1. Divide backing into 2 (1-yard) lengths. Join panels lengthwise. Seam will run horizontally.

2. Layer backing, batting, and quilt top; baste. Quilt as desired. Quilt shown was quilted with a looping line design in each row (Check out the Quilting Diagram).

3. Add binding to quilt.

Row Assembly Diagram

BTW: Lemme help!

Here are three ways kids can help out in the sewing room, even if they're not ready to sit at the machine:

1. Little ones can serenade you with a quilt-friendly version of "Old MacDonald." Help them identify items in the sewing room; e.g., stitches, patches, colors, thread, etc. "And on that quilt she had some thread; ee-i-ee-i-oh…"

2. Kids who can safely handle small scissors can help you snip apart long sections of chain piecing.

3. Involve kids in the design process. You can design the question to give them maximum satisfaction and still keep control of what you're working on, e.g., "Light gray thread or medium gray?"or "Do you like this green scrap or that one?"

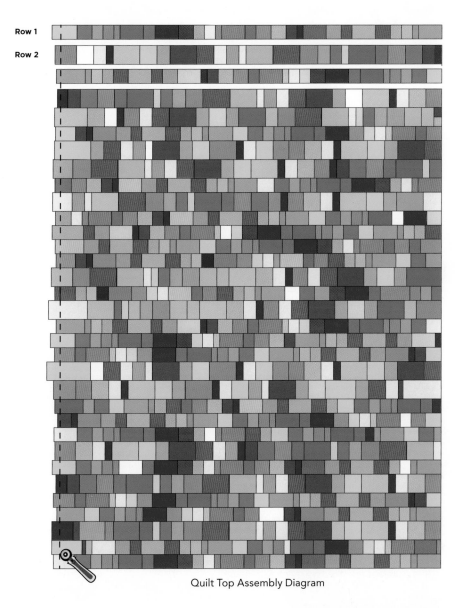

Row 1
Row 2

Quilt Top Assembly Diagram

Designer Profile

Amanda Jean Nyberg is an author, designer, and blogger who practically quilts in her sleep. She is co-author of *Sunday Morning Quilts* (Stash Books, 2012). Given the choice, she would use scraps over stash 9 times out of 10. Amanda can be found on the web at CrazyMomQuilts.blogspot.com, where you can read all about how she lives up to her blog name. She resides in Wisconsin with her husband and 3 kids.

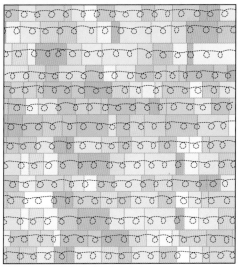

Quilting Diagram

5 Easy Pieces

Go, baby, go.
(The kids are alright.)

QUILT BY Colette Cogley
QUILTED BY Sally Evanshank

MATERIALS

1 yard brown print for blocks and border

½ yard yellow print for blocks and binding

1 fat quarter* blue print for blocks

1 fat quarter* green print for blocks

1 fat quarter* orange print for blocks

1½ yards backing fabric

Craft-size quilt batting

*Fat quarter = 18" × 20"

FABRIC NOTE:
Fabrics in the quilt shown
are from Michael Miller.

CUTTING

Measurements include ¼" seam allowances.

From brown print, first cut:

- 2 (6½"-wide) strips. Then, from those strips, cut 12 (6½") A squares.

- 4 (3½"-wide) strips. From these strips, cut 2 (3½" × 36½") side borders and 2 (3½" × 33½") top and bottom borders.

From yellow print, cut:

- 5 (2½"-wide) strips for binding.

- 2 (2"-wide) strips. From strips, cut 4 (2" × 9½") C rectangles and 4 (2" × 6½") B rectangles.

From your blue print, cut:

- 8 (2"-wide) strips. From strips, cut 8 (2" × 9½") C rectangles and 8 (2" × 6½") B rectangles.

From the green print, cut:

- 6 (2"-wide) strips. From strips, cut 6 (2" × 9½") C rectangles and 6 (2" × 6½") B rectangles.

And from the orange print, cut:

- 6 (2"-wide) strips. From strips, cut 6 (2" × 9½") C rectangles and 6 (2" × 6½") B rectangles.

MAKE IT YOUR OWN

Quelle feminine!

Striped fabric in the center = whoa!

BLOCK ASSEMBLY

1. Lay out 1 of your brown print A squares, 2 matching print B rectangles, and 2 matching print C rectangles. Look at the Block Assembly Diagram for help.

2. Join to complete 1 block (Block Diagram). Make 12 of these (easy!) blocks.

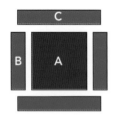

Block Assembly Diagram   Block Diagram

QUILT ASSEMBLY

1. Lay out blocks as shown in Quilt Top Assembly Diagram. Join your blocks into rows; join your rows to complete quilt center.

2. Add brown print side borders to quilt center. Then add top and bottom borders.

FINISHING

1. Layer backing, batting, and quilt top; baste. Quilt as desired. Quilt shown was quilted with a meandering straight line design (Quilting Diagram).

2. Join 2½"-wide yellow print strips into 1 continuous piece for straight-grain French-fold binding. Add binding to quilt.

ENJOY THE PROCESS

Buy a great set of colored pencils. Doodle. Sketch. Exercise your options.

Designer Profile

Colette Cogley is a quilter, educator, and the founder/owner of Quiltology: The Urban Quilt Space, in Chicago's Lincoln Park neighborhood. For more information about Colette and Quiltology, visit Quiltology.com.

BTW

BABY QUILT SAFETY

Follow these safety tips when you're making a quilt for a baby or young child:

• Do not use buttons, charms, or other embellishments on a quilt for a child under 3 years old; these small pieces could pose a choking hazard.

• Tying (as opposed to quilting) a baby quilt is okay, as long as ties are secure.

• For more information on safe bedding for babies, visit www.cpsc.gov

We show you how to fussy cut your fabrics!
HeyQuilty.com/FussyCut

Quilt Top Assembly Diagram

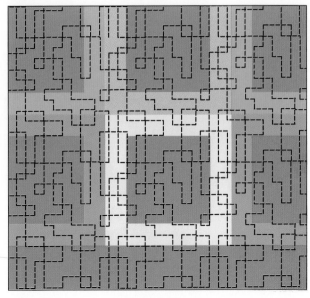

Quilting Diagram

Schoolgirl

This girl is a real smarty-pants.

QUILT BY Ebony Love

Watch the direction of your blocks!

MATERIALS

1 3/4 yards teal print for blocks and border

1 7/8 yards yellow print for blocks and binding

3/4 yard purple print for blocks

3/4 yard each of 2 cream prints for sashing and binding

3 fat eighths* assorted orange prints for sashing squares

4 yards backing fabric

Twin-size quilt batting

*Fat eighth = 9" × 20"

CUTTING

Measurements include 1/4" seam allowances. Border strips are exact length needed. You may want to cut them longer to allow for piecing variations.

From teal print, cut:
- 4 (6 7/8"-wide) strips. From strips, cut 16 (6 7/8") squares. Cut squares in half diagonally to make 32 half-square C triangles.

- 7 (4 1/2"-wide) strips. Piece strips to make 2 (4 1/2" × 66 1/2") top and bottom borders and 2 (4 1/2" × 58 1/2") side borders.

From yellow print, cut:
- 8 (3 7/8"-wide) strips. From strips, cut 80 (3 7/8") squares. Cut squares in half diagonally to make 160 half-square A triangles.

- 6 (3 1/2"-wide) strips. From strips, cut 64 (3 1/2") B squares.

- 4 (2 1/4"-wide) strips for binding.

From purple print, cut:
- 5 (3 7/8"-wide) strips. From strips, cut 48 (3 7/8") squares. Cut squares in half diagonally to make 96 half-square A triangles.

From each cream print, cut:
- 7 (2 1/2"-wide) strips. From strips, cut 20 (2 1/2" × 12 1/2") D rectangles.

- 2 (2 1/4"-wide) strips for binding.

From orange print fat eighths, cut a total of:
- 25 (2 1/2") E squares.

FABRIC NOTE:
Fabrics in the quilt shown are brought to you by Ebony Love's fabric stash!

BLOCK ASSEMBLY

1. Join 1 yellow print A triangle and 1 purple print A triangle as shown in Triangle-Square Diagrams. Make 96 of these triangle-squares.

Triangle-Square Diagrams

2. Lay out 1 triangle-square, 2 yellow print A triangles, and 1 teal print C triangle as shown in Unit 1 Diagrams. Join to complete 1 Unit 1. Make 32 of these Unit 1 pieces.

Unit 1 Diagrams

3. Lay out 2 triangle-squares and 2 yellow print B squares as shown in Unit 2 Diagrams. Join these into rows; then join rows to complete 1 Unit 2. Make 32 Unit 2.

Unit 2 Diagrams

4. Lay out 2 Unit 1 and 2 Unit 2 as shown in Block Assembly Diagram. Join into rows; join rows to complete 1 block (Block Diagram). Make 16 blocks, schoolgirl.

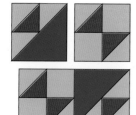

Block Assembly Diagram

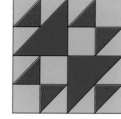

Block Diagram

QUILT ASSEMBLY

1. Lay out blocks, cream print D rectangles, and orange print E squares as shown in Quilt Top Assembly Diagram. Join into rows; join rows to complete quilt center.

2. Add teal print side borders to quilt center. Add teal print top and bottom borders to quilt.

FINISHING

1. Divide backing into 2 (2-yard) lengths. Cut 1 piece in half lengthwise to make 2 narrow panels. Join 1 narrow panel to each side of wider panel; press seam allowances toward narrow panels.

2. Layer backing, batting, and quilt top; baste. Quilt as desired. Quilt shown was freehand quilted with curved lines in blocks, with a dandelion design in sashing, and continuous flower designs in border using variegated thread (Quilting Diagram).

3. Join 2¼"-wide yellow print and cream print strips into 1 continuous piece for straight-grain French-fold binding. Add binding to quilt.

Designer Profile

Ebony Love is a designer, longarm quilter, and fabric die-cutting expert. She is well known for her video tutorials on YouTube, and recently launched a digital magazine, Blocks to Die For, especially for fabric die-cutting enthusiasts. For more information about Ebony, visit LoveBugStudios.com.

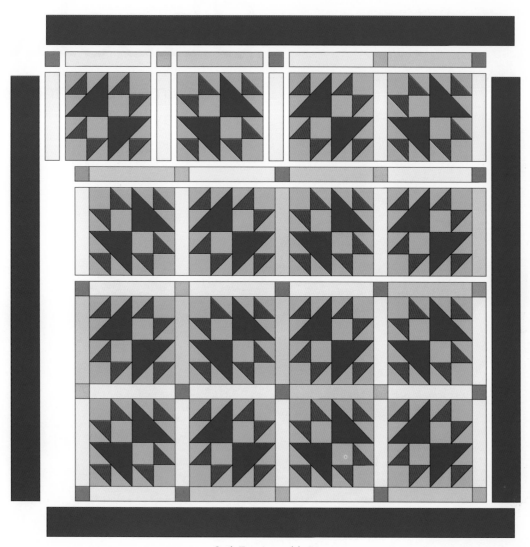

Quilt Top Assembly Diagram

Ebony is a frequent guest on Quilty...check her out!
HeyQuilty.com/Ebony

Quilting Diagram

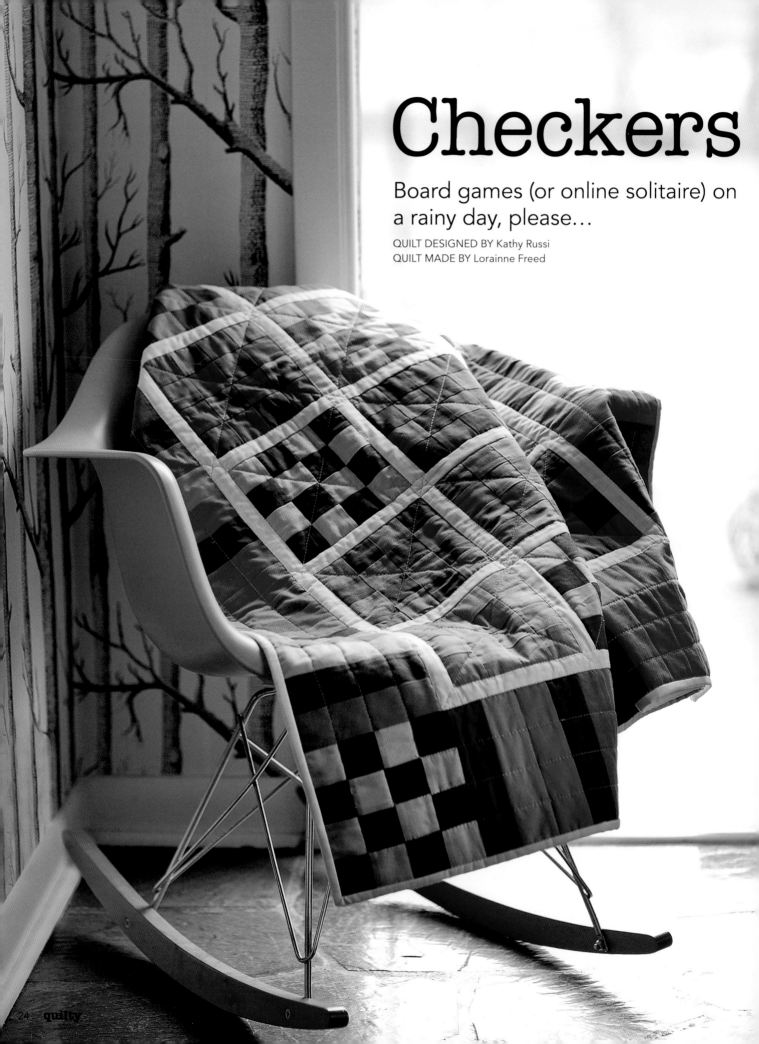

Checkers

Board games (or online solitaire) on a rainy day, please…

QUILT DESIGNED BY Kathy Russi
QUILT MADE BY Lorainne Freed

⭐ All these fabrics? Organic.

MATERIALS

20 fat quarters* assorted medium and dark solids for blocks and borders

1 yard cream solid for sashing and binding

3 yards backing fabric

Twin-size quilt batting

*Fat quarter = 18" × 20"

CUTTING

Measurements include ¼" seam allowances.

From each fat quarter, cut:
- 4 (2"-wide) strips for strip sets.
- 3 (2"-wide) strips. From strips, cut 6 (2" × 6½") border rectangles.

From cream solid, cut:
- 6 (2¼"-wide) strips for binding.
- 16 (1¼"-wide) strips. From strips, cut 8 (1¼" × 33½") horizontal sashing strips and 28 (1¼" × 6½") vertical sashing strips. Piece remaining strips to make 2 (1¼" × 48½") side inner borders.

SIZE OPTIONS

	Twin (66¾" × 93¾")	Full (90¼" × 90¾")
Blocks	100	124
Setting	8 × 12	10 × 12
MATERIALS		
Assorted medium & dark solids	50 fat quarters	62 fat quarters
Cream solid	2⅛ yards	2½ yards
Backing fabric	5½ yards	7½ yards
Batting	Full-size	Queen-size
CUTTING		
Border rectangles	184	202

FABRIC NOTE:
Fabrics in the quilt shown are from the Centennial solids collection by Judy Rothermel for Marcus.

BLOCK ASSEMBLY

1. Referring to Strip Set Diagram, join 2 pairs of matching 2"-wide strips to make 1 strip set. From strip set, cut 8 (2"-wide) segments.

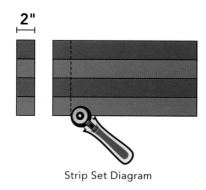

2"

Strip Set Diagram

2. Join 4 segments as shown in Block Assembly Diagram to complete 1 Sixteen Patch block (Block Diagram). Turn on your radio, favorite podcast, or streaming movie queue…and make 39 blocks.

Block Assembly Diagram   Block Diagram

QUILT ASSEMBLY

1. Lay out blocks and sashing strips as shown in Quilt Top Assembly Diagram. Join into rows; join rows to complete quilt center.

2. Add side inner borders to quilt center.

PIECED BORDER ASSEMBLY

1. Referring to Quilt Top Assembly Diagram, join 32 border rectangles to make 1 side outer border. Repeat for other side border. Add borders to quilt.

2. Just like you did in the previous step, join 23 border rectangles to make top border. Join 1 block to each end of top border. Repeat for bottom border. Add them to your stunning quilt.

FINISHING

1. Divide backing fabric into 2 (1½-yard) lengths. Join panels lengthwise. Your seam will run horizontally.

2. Layer backing, batting, and quilt top; baste. Quilt as desired. Quilt shown was machine quilted "in the ditch" around the blocks, with a diagonal grid through the blocks, and with parallel lines in the outer borders (Quilting Diagram).

3. Join 2¼"-wide cream strips into 1 continuous piece for straight-grain French-fold binding. Add binding to quilt.

Designer Profile

Kathy Russi particularly enjoys making scrap quilts. She chaired the Iowa Quilts Research Project, which documented pre-1925 quilts in the state. As a pharmacist, Kathy's professional career has included academia and pharmacy benefit management. She's been quilting for more than 30 years. To contact Kathy, email: KwRussi@aol.com.

ENJOY THE PROCESS

Is your cutting surface too low? Back pain and general aggravation can occur when you rotary cut hunched over a table. Take stock of your setup and if needed, tweak for maximum comfort.

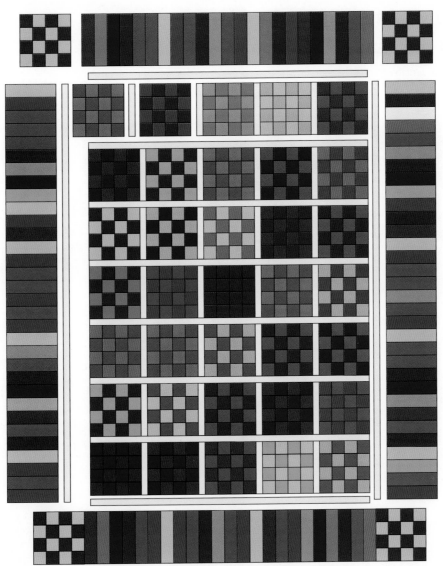

Quilt Top Assembly Diagram

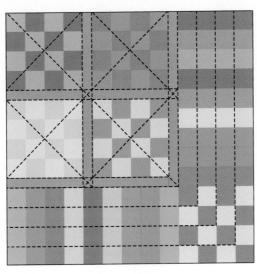

Quilting Diagram

Bell Bottoms

Like your favorite pair of jeans,
this quilt says, "Welcome home."

QUILT BY Jennifer Mathis

Let a splashy print shine in a wide border like this one.

MATERIALS

2 Design Rolls* or 36 (2$^{1}/_{2}$"-wide) strips

$^{3}/_{4}$ yard gold print for border

$^{5}/_{8}$ yard pink print for binding

3 yards backing fabric

Twin-size quilt batting

*Design Roll = 30 (2$^{1}/_{2}$"-wide) strips

CUTTING

Measurements include $^{1}/_{4}$" seam allowances. Border strips are exact length needed. You may want to cut them longer to allow for piecing variations.

From each of 3 (2$^{1}/_{2}$"-wide) strips, cut:
• 14 (2$^{1}/_{2}$") squares for Row 1.

From each of 6 (2$^{1}/_{2}$"-wide) strips, cut:
• 7 (2$^{1}/_{2}$") squares for Row 2.

From remaining 2$^{1}/_{2}$"-wide strips, cut a total of:
• 27 (2$^{1}/_{2}$" × 40$^{1}/_{2}$") strips.

From gold print, cut:
• 6 (4"-wide) strips. Piece strips to make 2 (4" × 62$^{1}/_{2}$") side borders and 2 (4" × 47$^{1}/_{2}$") top and bottom borders.

From pink print, cut:
• 7 (2$^{1}/_{4}$"-wide) strips for binding.

FABRIC NOTE:
Fabrics in the quilt shown are from the Bell Bottom collection by Jennifer Paganelli for Free Spirit.

QUILT ASSEMBLY

1. Join 20 squares, alternating 3 prints as shown in Row 1 Assembly Diagram. Make 2 Row 1. See how easy that was? Get ready to do it again...

Row 1 Assembly Diagram

2. Join 20 squares, alternating 6 prints as shown in Row 2 Assembly Diagram. Make 2 Row 2.

Row 2 Assembly Diagram

3. Lay out strips and rows as shown in Quilt Top Assembly Diagram. Join to complete quilt center.

FINISHING

1. Divide backing into 2 (1½-yard) lengths. Join pieces lengthwise. Seam will run horizontally.

2. Layer backing, batting, and quilt top; baste. Quilt as desired. Quilt shown was quilted with a diagonal grid (Quilting Diagram).

3. Join 2¼"-wide pink print strips into 1 continuous piece for straight-grain French-fold binding. Add binding to quilt.

Designer Profile

Jennifer Mathis is a self-taught sewist and quilter slightly obsessed with sewing, design, and modern fabric. She is driven by a need to express herself and a love of fabric and design. Jennifer shares her ideas, designs, projects, and interests on her blog, Ellison Lane Quilts. For more information about Jennifer, visit EllisonLane.blogspot.com.

SPOOLY SAYS:
"As you sew these strips of fabric, alternate at which end you begin sewing. This will keep your patchwork from stretching too much."

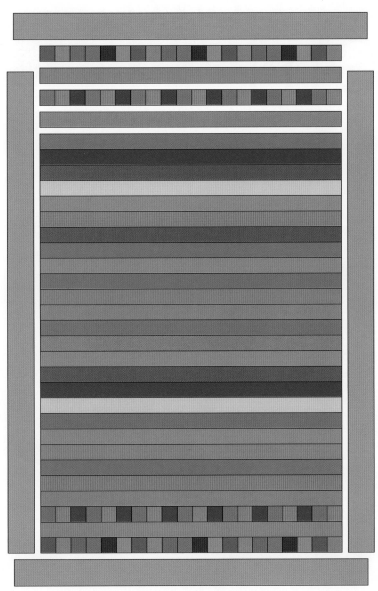

Quilt Top Assembly Diagram

Quilting Diagram

Dream Girl

Each patch represents another dream, another idea, another fresh start to the day.

QUILT BY Mary Fons • QUILTED BY Sally Evanshank

MATERIALS

20 fat quarters* assorted prints for blocks

4 yards soft pink solid for blocks, setting triangles and corner triangles

¾ yard black print for binding

7½ yards backing fabric

Full-size quilt batting

*Fat quarter = 18" × 20"

 NOTE: We're showing you how to do this quilt with just 20 fat quarters because we know that a lot of newer quilters don't have a bazillion different fabrics in their stashes—yet. If you do, then each individual square can be different. You make the call!

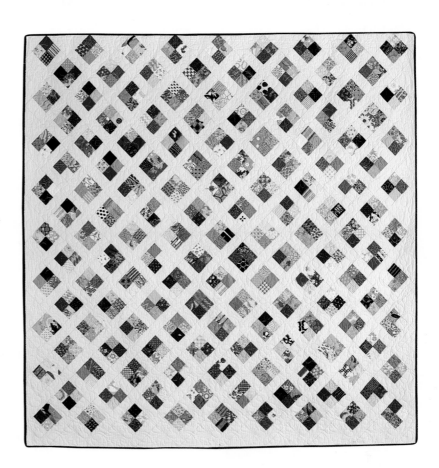

CUTTING

Measurements include ¼" seam allowances.

From each print fat quarter, cut:
• 5 (2½"-wide) strips. From strips, cut 29 (2½") A squares.

From soft pink solid, cut:
• 2 (9¾"-wide) strips. From strips, cut 8 (9¾") squares. Cut squares in half diagonally in both directions to make 32 side setting triangles.

• 1 (5⅛"-wide) strip. From strip, cut 2 (5⅛") squares. Cut squares in half diagonally to make 4 corner setting triangles.

• 44 (2½"-wide) strips. From strips, cut 145 (2½" × 4½") B rectangles and 145 (2½" × 6½") C rectangles.

From black print, cut:
• 9 (2¼"-wide) strips for binding.

FABRIC NOTE:
Pink fabric in the quilt shown is from Clothworks Everyday Organics. The patches were pulled from Mary's stash.

BLOCK ASSEMBLY

1. Referring to those handy Four Patch Unit Diagrams, join four A squares to make 1 Four Patch Unit. Make 145 Four Patch Units.

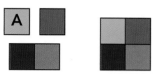

Four Patch Unit Diagrams

2. Lay out 1 Four Patch Unit, 1 pink solid B rectangle and 1 pink solid C rectangle as shown in Block Assembly Diagram. Join to complete 1 block (Block Diagram). Make 145 of these "charming" blocks.

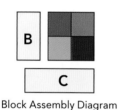

Block Assembly Diagram

Block Diagram

QUILT ASSEMBLY

1. Lay out blocks and setting triangles as shown in Quilt Top Assembly Diagram.

2. Join into diagonal rows; join rows to complete quilt top.

FINISHING

1. Divide backing into 3 (2½-yard) lengths. Cut 1 piece in half lengthwise to make 2 narrow panels. Join 1 narrow panel to each side of wider panel. (But of course, you can make your own backing any way you like. Improvising here is a good thing!) Remaining panel is extra and can be used to make a hanging sleeve.

2. Layer backing, batting, and quilt top; baste. Quilt as desired. Quilt shown was quilted with a leaf and swirl pattern (Quilting Diagram).

3. Join 2¼"-wide black print strips into 1 continuous piece for straight-grain French-fold binding. Add binding to quilt.

Designer Profile

In addition to hosting the weekly show on QNNtv.com, Mary edits *Quilty* magazine. She is co-host of *Love of Quilting* on PBS with her mom, Marianne Fons, and has the pleasure of interviewing quilt industry leaders on *Quilt With the Stars*. Mary enjoys traveling, shopping, eating, and dancing. She lives in downtown Chicago. For more information about Mary, visit MaryFons.com.

Backstory

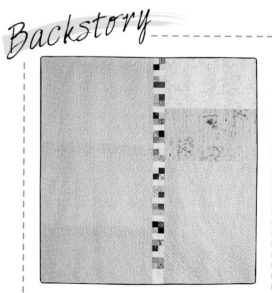

"Finding myself with leftover patches, I decided to run a series of them down the back. This provided a chance to get even more fabrics into my charm quilt, and I thought it would be a neat surprise. The other panel there was a large-scale print from Moda that I absolutely fell in love with. The fabric shows a little Red Riding Hood-like girl riding a horse, surrounded by little gnomes and deer…It fit the quilt's dreamy 'feel' perfectly." ~Mary

Quilt Top Assembly Diagram

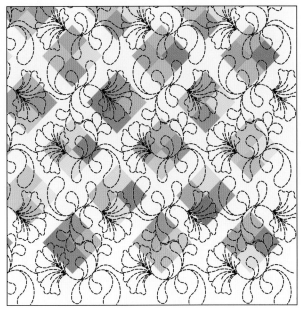

Quilting Diagram

Goose Parade

Honk if you like simple, fabulous quilts!

QUILT BY Mary Fons • MACHINE QUILTED BY Marianne Fons

MATERIALS

6 fat quarters* assorted prints in pink, blue, green, yellow, orange, and brown for Flying Geese Units

NOTE: For more variety, use more fabrics.

1¼ yards white print for Flying Geese Units

2 yards brown print for border

1⅞ yards light brown print for vertical rows

⅝ yard orange print for binding

Fons & Porter Flying Geese ruler (optional)

5 yards backing fabric

Twin-size quilt batting

*Fat quarter = 18" × 20"

FABRIC NOTE:
Fabrics in the quilt shown are primarily from Westminster Fabrics.

CUTTING

As usual, all measurements include ¼" seam allowances. Instructions are written for the Fons & Porter Flying Geese Ruler. This is a great tool and we recommend it, but it's not necessary—if you don't use it, follow cutting NOTES.

From those fabulous fat quarters, cut a total of:
- 24 (4"-wide) strips. From strips, cut 72 quarter-square A triangles.

NOTE: If not using the Fons & Porter Flying Geese Ruler, cut 9 (8¼"-wide) strips. From strips, cut 18 (8¼") squares. Cut squares in half diagonally in both directions to make 72 quarter-square A triangles.

From brown print, cut:
- 4 (10"-wide) **lengthwise** strips. From strips, cut 2 (10" × 68½") top and bottom borders and 2 (10" × 63½") side borders.

From white print, cut:
- 11 (4"-wide) strips. From strips, cut 144 half-square B triangles.

NOTE: If not using the Fons & Porter Flying Geese Ruler, cut 8 (4⅜"-wide) strips. From strips, cut 72 (4⅜") squares. Cut squares in half diagonally to make 144 half-square B triangles.

From light brown print, cut:
- 3 (7½"-wide) **lengthwise** strips. From strips, cut 3 (7½" × 63½") vertical rows.

From orange print, cut:
- 8 (2¼"-wide) strips for binding.

FLYING GEESE UNIT ASSEMBLY

1. Lay out 1 print A triangle and 2 white print B triangles as shown in Flying Geese Unit Diagrams.
2. Join triangles to complete 1 Flying Geese Unit. Make 72 Flying Geese Units.

Flying Geese Unit Diagrams

QUILT ASSEMBLY

1. Lay out 18 Flying Geese Units as shown in Quilt Top Assembly Diagram. Join to make 1 Flying Geese row. Make 4 of these rows.

2. Join your Flying Geese rows and light brown print rows as shown to complete quilt center.

3. Add brown print side borders to quilt center. Add brown print top and bottom borders to quilt. That's it, kid!

FINISHING

1. Divide backing into 2 (2½-yard) lengths. Cut 1 piece in half lengthwise to make 2 narrow panels. Join 1 narrow panel to each side of wider panel; press seam allowances toward narrow panels.

2. Layer backing, batting, and quilt top; baste. Quilt as desired. Quilt shown was quilted in the ditch in Flying Geese Units and with allover meandering in border (Quilting Diagram).

3. Join 2¼"-wide orange print strips into 1 continuous piece for straight-grain French-fold binding. Add binding to quilt.

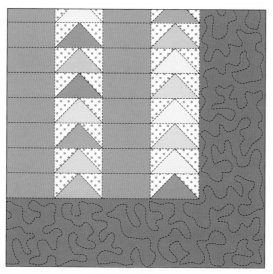

Quilting Diagram

Quilt Top Assembly Diagram

Blonde Redhead

This quilt might be your new best friend.

QUILT BY Mary Fons

MATERIALS

17 fat quarters* assorted prints in gold and blue

1¼ yards white solid

6 yards red solid

¾ yard black solid for binding

7⅞ yards backing fabric

Queen-size quilt batting

*Fat quarter = 18" × 20"

CUTTING

Measurements include ¼" seam allowances.

From each print fat quarter, cut:
- 6 (2½"-wide) strips. From strips, cut 36 (2½") squares.

From white solid, cut:
- 4 (6½"-wide) strips. From strips, cut 49 (6½" × 2½") rectangles.
- 7 (2½"-wide) strips. From strips, cut 98 (2½") squares.

From red solid, cut:
- 7 (10½"-wide) strips. From strips, cut 112 (10½" × 2½") sashing strips.
- 13 (6½"-wide) strips. From strips, cut 196 (6½" × 2½") rectangles.
- 17 (2½"-wide) strips. From strips, cut 260 (2½") squares.

From black solid, cut:
- 10 (2¼"-wide) strips for binding.

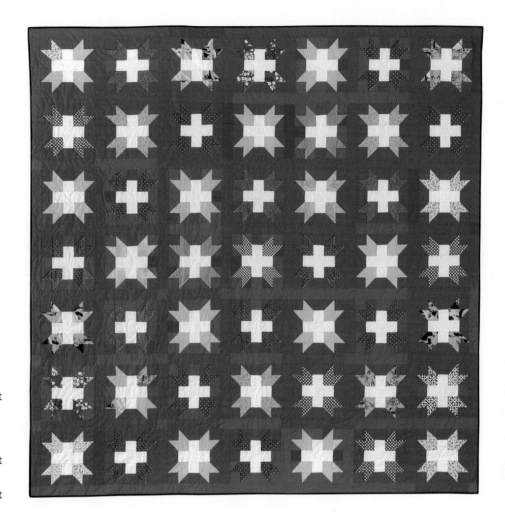

FABRIC NOTE:
Fabrics in the quilt shown are brought to you by Mary Fons' fabric stash!

SPOOLY SAYS:

"The more quilts you make, the better you get at making them. Be patient & keep sewing! And take classes in shops or online. (DailyCraftTV.com is a great web site for online classes...) You can do it!"

BLOCK ASSEMBLY

1. See those little Diagonal Seams Diagrams down there? That's what we'll do first. Take it slow. You'll get this quickly—we'll start with a blue block. Place 1 blue print square face-down on the red solid rectangle. Using your sewing machine, stitch diagonally from corner to corner, just like it shows you.

Diagonal Seams Diagrams

2. Measuring ¼" from the line you just sewed, trim off the extra. Press the piece open to reveal the new blue corner of your rectangle! Now repeat that on the other side. That's a Diagonal Seams Unit. You'll need four of those for one block. Good job.

3. Check out the Block Center Diagrams down there. Here's what you do: Lay out 4 matching blue print squares, 2 white solid squares, and 1 white solid rectangle, just like it shows you. Just join the rows together! Go from left to right—one piece to the next till you have three complete rows. Then join the rows to make that center patch.

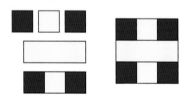

Block Center Diagrams

4. Okay, so lay out your Block Center, your 4 Diagonal Seams Units, and 4 red solid squares like it shows you in the Block Assembly Diagrams. It's time to join rows again! Join one row, then the next, and the next. Then join the rows to complete the block.

 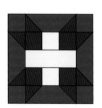 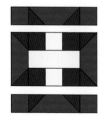

Block Assembly Diagrams   Block Diagram

5. Make a whole bunch more of those. (48 more, to be exact. Whee!)

6. Add 1 red solid sashing strip to the left side of each block as shown in the Pre-Sashing Diagram.

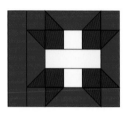

Pre-Sashing Diagram

QUILT ASSEMBLY

1. Join 7 sashing strips and 8 red solid squares to make 1 sashing row, like it shows you in the Quilt Top Assembly Diagram, opposite. Don't be scared; it's a long row, but if you take your time and concentrate, you'll be fine.

2. Lay out your blocks, sashing rows, and remaining sashing strips. Join your rows, then join the completed rows to other completed rows and, voila! You just made a quilt top.

FINISHING

1. You need a back on your quilt, of course. Here's what you do: Divide your backing fabric into 3 (2⅝-yard = 94½") lengths. Cut 1 piece in half lengthwise to make 2 narrow panels. Join 1 wider panel to each side of 1 narrow panel. Press seam allowances toward the narrow panel. The remaining panel? Save it for something else later.

2. Layer backing fabric, batting, and quilt top. Either send your quilt to a longarmer (if sending it to the longarm quilter, don't layer), or tackle the quilting yourself. We did circles and spirals on this one and the Quilting Diagram may give you ideas.

3. Bind your quilt! We used a black binding for this one, but it's up to you. Binding can be a little intimidating, but never fear: we can help. For more detailed binding instructions go to **FonsandPorter.com/Binding** and then just go for it. It doesn't have to be perfect, especially if you're brand new to all this.

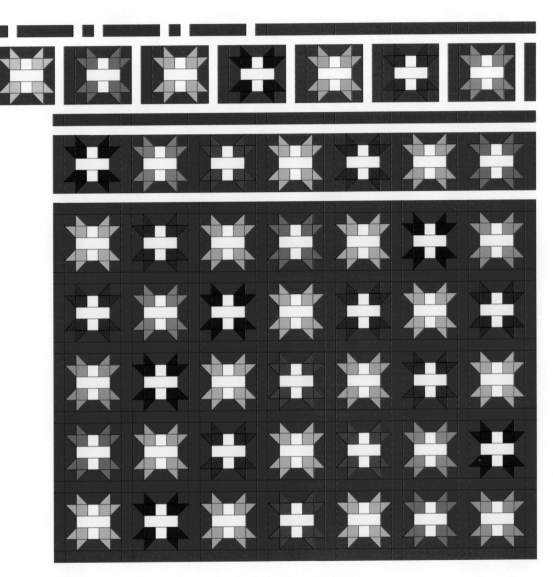

Quilt Top Assembly Diagram

Mary and her sister Rebecca Fons construct this block on Quilty!
HeyQuilty.com/Blonde

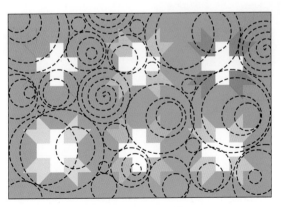

Quilting Diagram

A Game Of Hearts

You don't need
curved seams
to feel the love.

QUILT BY Cindy Carter

MATERIALS

11 fat quarters* medium/dark pink and red prints and solids for blocks

½ yard each of 14 light pink prints and solids for blocks and sashing

⅞ yard of pink stripe for binding

4½ yards 60″-wide backing fabric

Full-size quilt batting

*Fat quarter = 18″ × 20″

NOTE: This quilt is backed with short pile Minky fabric to make it snuggly soft.

CUTTING

Measurements include ¼″ seam allowances.

From each medium/dark fat quarter, cut:
• 5 (2″-wide) strips. From strips, cut 15 (2″ × 3½″) B rectangles and 15 (2″) A squares.

From each light ½-yard piece, cut:
• 2 (3½″-wide) strips. From strips, cut 16 (3½″ × 5″) D rectangles.
• 2 (3¼″-wide) strips. From strips, cut 24 (3¼″) squares. Cut squares in half diagonally to make 48 half-square C triangles.
• 1 (2″-wide) strip. From strip, cut 12 (2″) A squares.

From pink stripe, cut:
• 9 (2¼″-wide) bias strips. Join strips to make bias binding.

FABRIC NOTE: Fabrics in the quilt shown are from Cindy's collection.

NOTE: You will have a few A squares, B rectangles, C triangles, and D rectangles left over, which you can save for another quilt.

BLOCK ASSEMBLY

1. Join 1 light A square, 1 medium/dark A square, and 1 medium/dark B rectangle as shown in Center Unit Diagrams. Make 162 Center Units.

Center Unit Diagrams

2. Lay out 1 Center Unit and 4 light C triangles as shown in Heart Unit Diagrams. Center and sew 2 triangles to opposite sides of Center Unit. Trim corners of C triangles even with Center Unit.

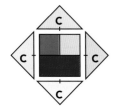 

Heart Unit Diagrams

3. Now, join remaining C triangles to Center Unit to complete 1 Heart Unit. Make 162 Heart Units.

4. Lay out 4 Heart Units as shown in Block Assembly Diagram. Join into rows; join rows to complete 1 block (Block Diagram). Make 30 blocks.

  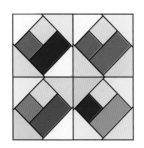

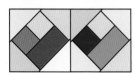

Block Assembly Diagram   Block Diagram

QUILT ASSEMBLY

1. Join 3 light D rectangles as shown in Sashing Unit Diagram. Make 71 Sashing Units.

2. Lay out blocks, Sashing Units, and remaining Heart Units as shown in Quilt Top Assembly Diagram.

3. Join into rows; join rows to complete quilt top.

Sashing Unit Diagram

FINISHING

1. Divide backing into 2 (2¼-yard) lengths. Join panels lengthwise. Seam allowance will run horizontally.

2. Layer backing, batting, and quilt top; baste. Quilt as desired. Quilt shown was quilted in the ditch (Quilting Diagram).

3. Add binding to quilt

Designer Profile

Cindy Carter has been making quilts since 2000. She says, "Making and sharing my original patterns allows me to give back in gratitude for all my many blessings." For more information about Cindy, visit: CarterQuilter.wordpress.com.

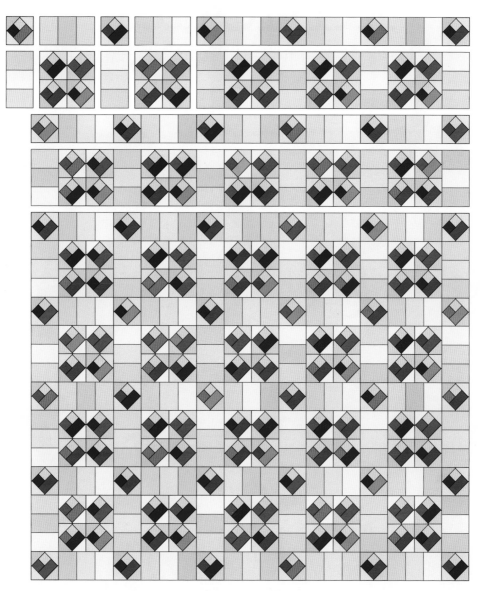

Quilt Top Assembly Diagram

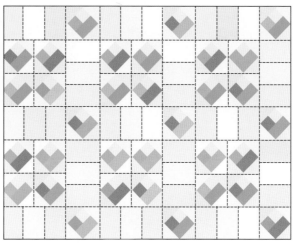

Quilting Diagram

Amelia

It's a bird! It's a plane! Okay, it's definitely a plane!

QUILT BY Quilty & Co.
MADE AND QUILTED BY TailorMade by Design

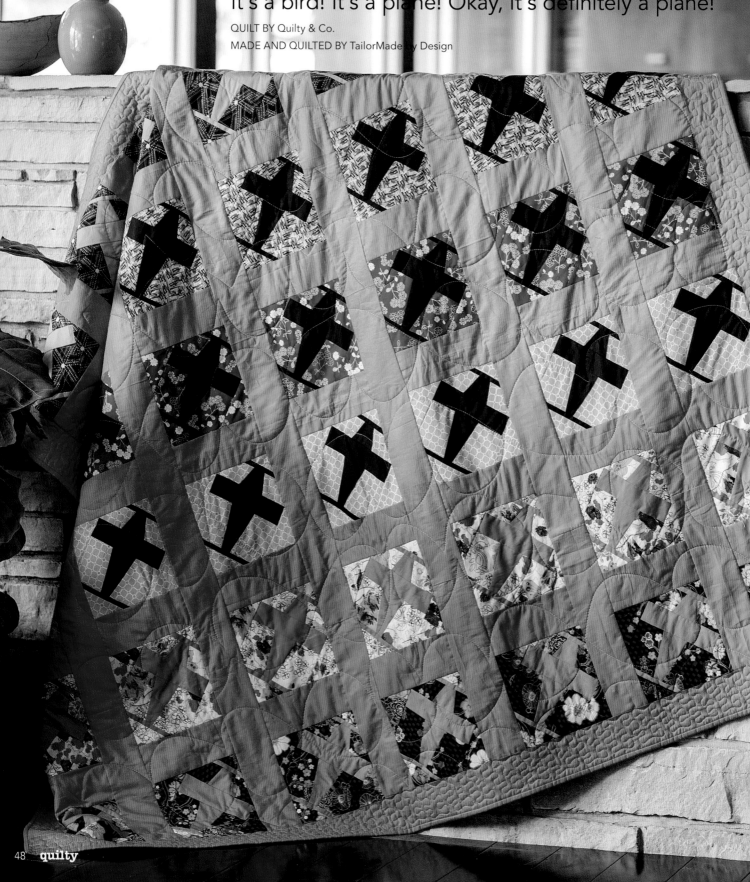

MATERIALS

3½ yards pink solid for sashing, borders, and binding

¾ yard green solid for blocks

1 yard black solid for blocks

¾ yard blue solid for blocks

¾ yard each of 6 assorted prints for blocks

Paper for foundation piecing

4½ yards backing fabric

Twin-size quilt batting

FABRIC NOTE: Airplane blocks made with Art Gallery Prints.

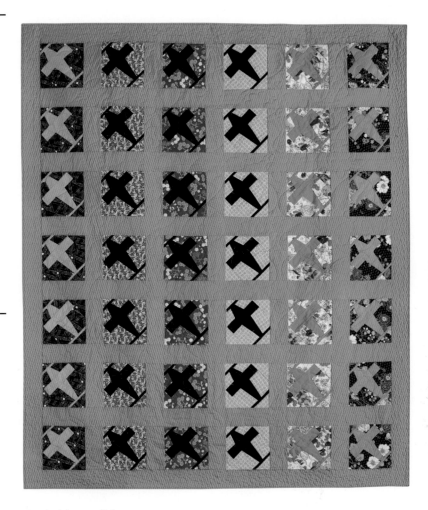

CUTTING

Measurements include ¼" seam allowances. Patterns for foundations are on page 52. Pieces for foundation piecing are cut oversize.

From pink solid, cut:
- 7 (3½"-wide) strips. From strips, cut 35 (3½" × 7½") vertical sashing rectangles.

- 8 (2¼"-wide) strips for binding.

From remainder of pink solid, cut:
- 10 (3½"-wide) **lengthwise** strips. From strips, cut 6 (3½" × 57½") horizontal sashing rectangles, 2 (3½" × 67½") side borders, and 2 (3½" × 63½") top and bottom borders.

From your green solid, cut the following:
- 14 (3" × 5") rectangles for foundation piecing (A1).

- 14 (2½" × 6½") rectangles for foundation piecing (A6).

- 14 (2½") squares for foundation piecing (B1).

- 14 (1" × 5½") rectangles for foundation piecing (A4).

- 14 (1" × 4½") rectangles for foundation piecing (B4).

From your black solid, cut:
- 21 (3" × 5") rectangles for foundation piecing (A1).

- 21 (2½" × 6½") rectangles for foundation piecing (A6).

- 21 (2½") squares for foundation piecing (B1).

- 21 (1" × 5½") rectangles for foundation piecing (A4).

- 21 (1" × 4½") rectangles for foundation piecing (B4).

From blue solid, cut:
- 7 (3" × 5") rectangles for foundation piecing (A1).

- 7 (2½" × 6½") rectangles for foundation piecing (A6).

- 7 (2½") squares for foundation piecing (B1).

- 7 (1" × 5½") rectangles for foundation piecing (A4).

- 7 (1" × 4½") rectangles for foundation piecing (B4).

From each ¾ yard piece, cut:
- 7 (4½") squares. Cut squares in half diagonally to make 14 half-square triangles for foundation piecing (A7 and A8).

- 4 (4") squares. Cut squares in half diagonally to make 7 half-square triangles for foundation piecing (A5).

- 14 (3½" × 4½") rectangles for foundation piecing (A2 and A3).

- 14 (3½" × 2½") rectangles for foundation piecing (pieces B2 and B3).

- 4 (3") squares. Cut squares in half diagonally to make 7 half-square triangles for foundation piecing (B5).

BLOCK ASSEMBLY

1. Trace or photocopy 42 each of Foundation Units A and B from patterns on page 52.

2. Referring to Block Unit Diagrams, paper piece foundation units in numerical order. Make 6 sets of 7 matching Unit A. Make 6 sets of 7 matching Unit B.

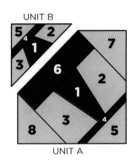

Block Unit Diagram

3. Lay out 1 Unit A and 1 matching Unit B as shown in Block Assembly Diagram. Join to complete 1 block (Block Diagram). Make 42 blocks.

 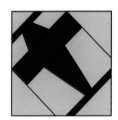

Block Assembly Diagram   Block Diagram

QUILT ASSEMBLY

1. Lay out blocks and pink sashing rectangles as shown in Quilt Top Assembly Diagram.

2. Join into rows; join rows to complete quilt center.

3. Add side borders to quilt center. Add top and bottom borders to quilt.

FINISHING

1. Divide backing into 2 (2¼-yard) lengths. Cut 1 piece in half to make 2 narrow panels. Join 1 narrow panel to each side of wider panel; press seam allowances toward narrow panels.

2. Layer backing, batting, and quilt top; baste. Quilt as desired. Quilt shown was quilted with an all over cloud design in quilt center and meandering in border (Quilting Diagram).

3. Join 2¼"-wide pink strips into 1 continuous piece for straight-grain French-fold binding. Add binding to quilt. Fly into sky.

Designer Profile

Quilty magazine is dedicated to bringing you gorgeous quilts that you can actually make. We believe in quilts that make people smile. For more information about Quilty, visit: HeyQuilty.com.

MAKE IT YOUR OWN

We ♥ this block!!

Follow along as we make this block!
HeyQuilty.com/Amelia

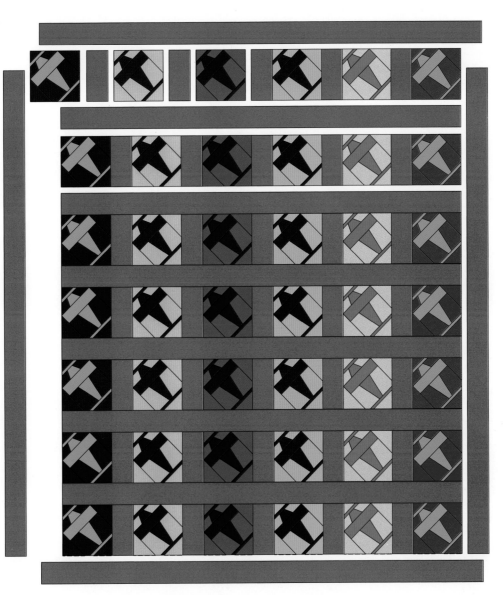

Quilt Top Assembly Diagram

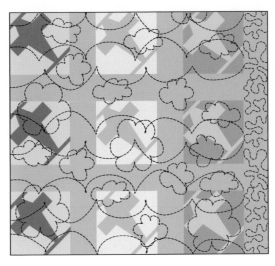

Quilting Diagram

Amelia

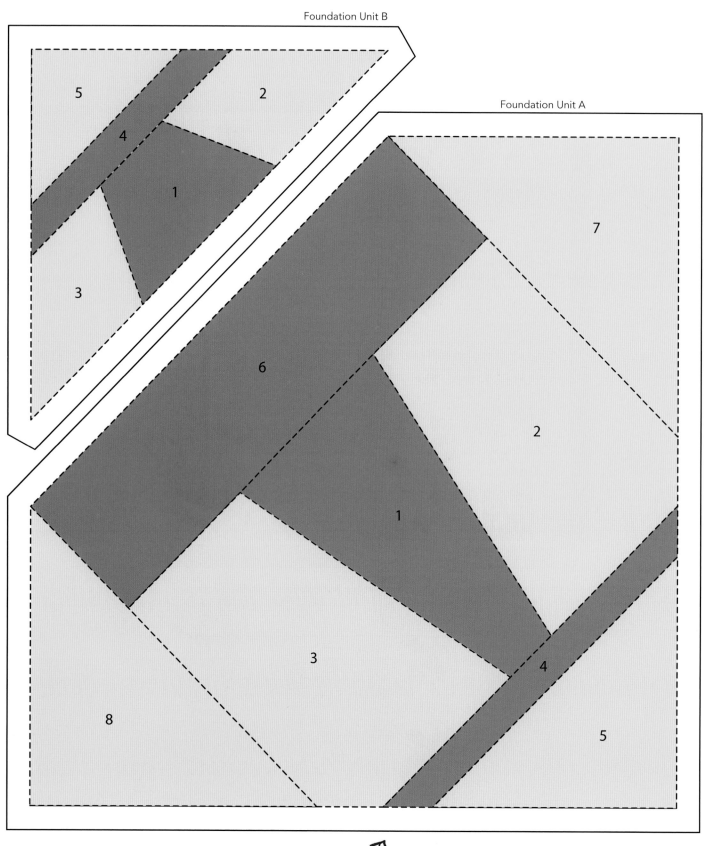

Foundation Unit B

Foundation Unit A

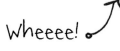

Wheeee!

Balancing the Scales
Working with Small- and Large-Scale Prints

By Ellen Rushman

It's a common rookie experience: The fabric you lovingly, painstakingly selected gets sliced up for your patchwork and the result is…not good. This is not because you can't pick beautiful fabric! Nine times out of ten, you have a scale problem.

SCALE AND WHY IT MATTERS

"Scale" is the relative size of the design on a piece of printed fabric. This is typically measured in square inches. A fabric with 10 polka dots per square inch would be considered a "small scale" print—that's a lotta dots. A floral fabric with petals that measure 3" across? Large scale, definitely. And since scale covers a spectrum, there's everything in between these examples, too!

If you slice up a flower that measures 3" across into 2½" strips, you'll get some sections of the strip that are all flower, some that look ½ flower, and some sections that might not "catch" any flower at all. This can cause trouble because pieces cut from that strip won't be a consistent color. In quilts, this can make the difference between a successful quilt block and a muddy, funky one.

THE RULES, LOOSELY

1 To put it really, really broadly: Use small prints for small patchwork and large prints for larger patchwork. A 4" finished block will yield no surprises when made with teeny prints; a 6" wide border will give ample room for large-scale prints to shine, intact.

2 Since large-scale prints lend themselves to larger pieces within a quilt, try using big pieces of large-scale fabric; your project will be finished in no time. Remember this next time you are in a quilting time crunch.

3 Solid fabrics are all the rage these days. Small-scale prints can function as read-as-solids within a quilt. Often called "blenders" these fabrics add depth to your project. Experiment!

4 Scale doesn't always read correctly on a computer. Before you "add to cart," think about the size of the swatch you are looking at on the screen. Some online stores have scale clearly marked while others don't.

5 Mix it up. Use small and large scale prints together in the same quilt. This creates intrigue, movement, and dimension.

6 If all else fails, fussy cut. We all have that print with one cool part every eight inches surrounded by a bunch of weird stuff, right? Cut out what you want from the fabric and ditch the rest.

7 Most people use color as their category of choice for fabric organization. Maybe give scale a try: separate in terms of small, medium, and large, and then by color. As you audition fabric for a project, think about the relationship between the size of the piece and the scale of your print.

8 If you need a 4" square in your project, cut a 4" square window out of a piece of cardboard. Move the window around the fabric you are thinking of using. Does it work? You decide, it's your quilt!

9 Be aware of the repeat on large-scale fabrics. Say you're cutting strips from a large-scale print with flowers in a linear formation. Each strip ends up with a stripe of flowers. As you cut the strip into squares, each square has a flower in it. Do you want each piece to look the same? Alter your cutting pattern if you want to create a random effect of the flowers within your pieces.

10 Don't take these rules too seriously. You are a quilter: buy the fabric you like. Keep it up, build your stash. Use these tips to match the right fabric to the right project and happy stitching!

HeyQuilty.com/Scales is a nice video tutorial...check it out!

11 Essential Tools for Quilters

If you want to make an omelet, you'll have to go to a store (or a chicken!) and get some eggs. Patchwork requires supplies, too. Here's a basic list for anyone who thinks she might like to cut up big pieces of fabric into small pieces of fabric and sew them together again.

1 SEWING MACHINE

We live in a world full of sewing machines that would make your great-grandmother weep with joy. Quilty highly recommends visiting a certified sewing machine dealer. Whether it's your first machine or your third, a dealer can answer questions, do repairs, and help "fit" you with one of the best friends you'll ever have.

2 FABRIC

Cotton fabric is best: don't try to make a quilt out of grandma's hankies your first time out. A great quilt shop will help you find what you like and steer you away from inexpensive, flimsy fabrics and into the world of luxurious quilting-grade cotton.

3 ROTARY CUTTER, RULER, & MAT

There are many ways to cut fabric, but the vast majority of quilters today use the rotary cutting system. The rotary cutter is essentially a razor blade on a wheel; the ruler (start with a 6" × 24") offers an edge against which to cut; the mat (24" × 36" is best) protects your table and your blade. A quilt shop will have these items on hand and can help you understand how to use them safely.

4 IRON & IRONING BOARD

Making patchwork is three things: cutting, sewing, and pressing. Pressing your patchwork sets your seams and crisps up the units and blocks. Get a good iron and a safe pressing surface, and always unplug your iron when you're done.

5 SEAM RIPPER

Nobody's perfect.

6 DESIGN WALL

If you were painting, you'd want to step back from time to time and see the whole picture. It's the same with patchwork. A design wall is a place for your patchwork so you can see what's happening. A large piece of white flannel or thin quilt batting tacked up will do; there are also pre-made design walls available.

7 PINS & PINCUSHION

Thin, glass head pins are essential for basic patchwork. You'll be using them to hold units and rows in place.

8 SCISSORS

We really believe you need two kinds of scissors at your sewing table: a pair of large shears and a smaller pair of thread cutting/snipping scissors. When you get them, use them only for cutting fabric and thread—no cardboard boxes, crafting papers, etc.

9 A PATTERN

Your pattern is your GPS, your quilt recipe. Find the one that speaks to you in a magazine, online, from a book, or a friend...and refer to it often.

10 THREAD

Thread comes in an endless number of colors as well as different weights, textures, and material types. Depending on what you're sewing, quilting, embroidering, etc., you'll want different types of thread. For basic patchwork, look for a thread that reads 50/3 (this refers to the weight and yarn count) in the color of your choice.

11 TIME

It's hard to make a quilt if you're not sewing. Make time for yourself and your hobby. Creative pursuits feed us in all kinds of ways; working on a quilt can actually make you feel like you have more time for everything else.

We go over needed supplies in this Quilty video:
HeyQuilty.com/Supplies

Making a Design Wall

At Quilty, we feel a design wall is as essential to the quilt making process as fabric. To really "see" what you're doing and track your progress, a design wall is an invaluable tool that allows you to tack up blocks and pieces as you go. Your quilts will never be the same—they'll be better.

1. Make friends with someone who owns a truck.

2. Get a piece of foam insulation board from the hardware store. Get it home in your friend's truck. Most insulation boards come in 4' × 8' sheets. Cut to size as needed with a craft knife or box cutter (**Photo A**).

3. Cover with a neutral colored felt; secure with T-pins. You'd think staples would work, but they don't. Trust us. (**Photos B & C**).

4. Prop against wall or secure onto wall however you see fit. Throw those blocks and pieces up there and go, baby, go! (**Photos D & E**).

Felt!

It's me, SPOOLY!

HeyQuilty.com/Wall has a great step-by-step video tutorial!

Boot Camp

SNIP SLICE CUT

Accurate Cutting: **Fear not!**

Measure twice, cut once is good advice. Any quilter who has sliced incorrectly through a piece of fabric she can't replace knows this all too well. Measuring and cutting accurately are important for successful quilting, so learn how to be great at it. It takes practice.

Cutting for patchwork usually begins with cutting strips, which are then cut into smaller pieces.

First, cut straight strips from a fat quarter:

1. Fold fat quarter in half with selvage edge at the top (**Photo A**).

2. Straighten the edge of your fabric by placing your ruler atop fabric, aligning one of the lines on ruler with selvage edge of fabric (**Photo B**). Cut along right edge of ruler. Make sure you a) wear your safety glove and b) press firmly, with commitment, all the way from edge to edge for a clean cut.

3. Rotate fabric, and use ruler to measure from cut edge to desired strip width (**Photo C**). Measurements in instructions include ¼" seam allowances. After cutting the required number of strips, cut strips into squares or rectangles as needed.

Don't forget to use a safety glove when cutting. Save those fingers...

 NOTE: Cut strips across the fabric width unless directed otherwise. We're using the rotary cutting system in this lesson.

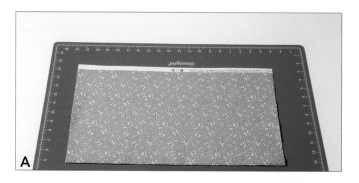

A

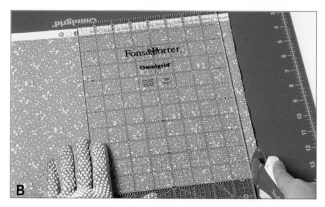

B

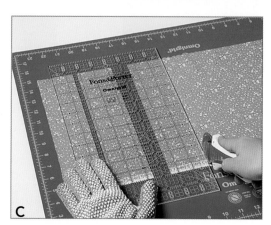

C

 Video alert! We walk you through how to check your patchwork.
HeyQuilty.com/SeamTest

# Boot Camp

Cutting Half-Square Triangles

With a Fons & Porter Half & Quarter Ruler, you can easily cut half-square triangles from strips. How cool is that?!

FOR HALF-SQUARE TRIANGLES:

1. Straighten the left edge of fabric strip. Place the line of the Fons and Porter Half & Quarter Ruler that corresponds with your strip width on the bottom edge of strip, aligning left edge of ruler with straightened edge of strip. The yellow tip of ruler will extend beyond top edge of strip.

2. Cut along right edge of ruler to make 1 half-square triangle (**Photo A**).

3. Turn ruler and align same line with top edge of strip. Cut along right edge of ruler (**Photo B**).

4. Repeat to cut required number of half-square triangles.

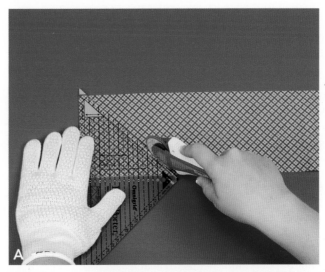

A

 You will get the hang of it and then you will <u>love</u> this method!

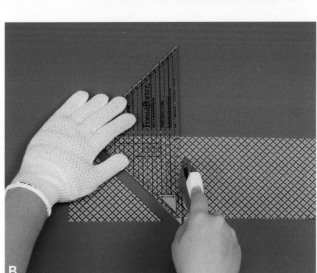

B

...why don't we call this "Quilty High Heels Camp" instead?

Note! This ruler helps you cut HSTs <u>and</u> QSTs. Make sure you're using the "Yellow" side this time.

We walk you through HST's here!
HeyQuilty.com/HST

Boot Camp

Easy Machine Quilting:
Yes you can!

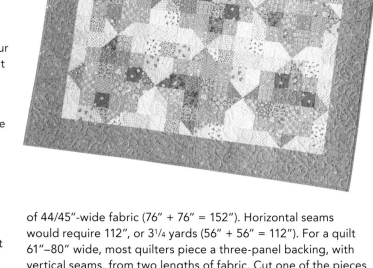

There's a little saying among quilters, "There are three ways to quilt a quilt: by hand, by machine…or by check." Some of us enjoy making quilt tops so much, we prefer to hire a professional machine quilter (usually a "longarmer") to finish our work. But if you'd rather tackle the job yourself, super! The Split NinePatch baby quilt shown has simple machine quilting you can definitely handle.

Decide what color thread will look best on your quilt top before choosing your backing fabric. A thread color that will blend in with the quilt top is a good choice for beginners because mistakes won't show as much. (Choose backing fabric that will blend with your thread, too—prints are a good choice.)

WHICH WIDTH IS WHICH?

The backing fabric must be at least 3"–4" larger than your quilt top on all 4 sides. So, say your quilt top measures 44" × 44". Your backing needs to be at least 50" × 50". If your quilt top is 80" × 96", then your backing fabric needs to be at least 86" × 102". You get the idea.

For quilt tops 36" wide or less, use a single width of fabric for the backing. Buy enough length to allow adequate margin at quilt edges, as noted above. When your quilt is wider than 36", one option is to use 60"-, 90"-, or 108"-wide fabric for the quilt backing. Because fabric selection is limited for wide fabrics, quilters generally piece the quilt backing from 44/45"-wide fabric, which just means that they sew multiple pieces of fabric together. Plan on 40"–42" of usable fabric width when estimating how much fabric to buy.

For a quilt 37"–60" wide, a backing with horizontal seams is usually the most economical use of fabric. For example, for a quilt 50" × 70", vertical seams would require 152", or 4¼ yards,

of 44/45"-wide fabric (76" + 76" = 152"). Horizontal seams would require 112", or 3¼ yards (56" + 56" = 112"). For a quilt 61"–80" wide, most quilters piece a three-panel backing, with vertical seams, from two lengths of fabric. Cut one of the pieces in half lengthwise, and sew the halves to opposite sides of the wider panel. Press the seams away from the center panel.

For a quilt 81"–120" wide, you will need three lengths of fabric, plus extra margin. For example, for a quilt 108" × 108", purchase at least 342", or 9½ yards, of 44/45"-wide fabric (114" + 114" + 114" = 342").

For a three-panel backing, pin the selvage edge of the center panel to the selvage edge of the side panel, with edges aligned and right sides facing. Machine stitch with a ½" seam. Trim seam allowances to ¼", trimming off the selvages from both panels at once. Press the seam away from the center of the quilt. Repeat on other side of center panel.

For a two-panel backing, join panels in the same manner as above, and press the seam to one side.

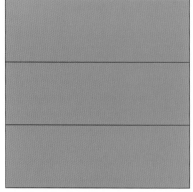

Horizontal Seam Back

Three-Panel Backing

Offset Seam

(YUM)

MAKE YOURSELF A SANDWICH

Create a "quilt sandwich" by layering your backing, batting, and quilt top. Find the crosswise center of the backing fabric by folding it in half. Mark with a pin on each side. Lay backing down on a table or floor, "right side down." Tape corners and edges of backing to the surface with masking or painter's tape so that backing is taut but not pulled so tight it bags anywhere. (Photo A).

Fold batting in half crosswise and position it atop backing fabric, centering folded edge at center of backing (Photo B). Unfold batting and smooth it out atop backing (Photo C).

What exactly is a quilt?!
HeyQuilty.com/Sandwich

In the same manner, fold the quilt top in half crosswise and center it atop backing and batting (Photo D). Unfold top and smooth it out on top of your batting (Photo E).

Use safety pins to pin baste the layers (Photo F). Pins should be placed about a fist-width apart. (Psst…A grapefruit spoon makes closing the pins easier. Try it!)

For straight line quilting, install an even feed or walking foot on your machine. This presser foot helps all three layers of your quilt move through the machine evenly without bunching.

An easy way to quilt your first quilt is to stitch "in the ditch" along seam lines. No marking is needed for this type of quilting. Enjoy machine quilting, folks! It's fun stuff.

life is good w/a walking foot…

by far the easiest method… a good place to start.

Walking Foot

Stitching "in the ditch"

Boot Camp

Binding 101

We like this method for attaching binding to the edge of your quilt. Observe other quilters, ask questions, watch videos, and in no time, binding will be no biggie.

PREPARING BINDING

Strips for quilt binding may be cut either on the straight of grain or on the bias. For this demo, cut strips on the straight of grain.

1. Measure the perimeter of your quilt and add approximately 24" to allow for mitered corners and finished ends.

2. Cut the necessary number of strips to achieve desired length. We like to cut binding strips 2¼" wide, but some like 2½". It's your choice.

3. Join your strips into 1 continuous piece using diagonal seams (**Photo A**). Press the seams open.

4. Press your binding in half lengthwise, wrong sides facing, to make French-fold binding (**Photo B**).

ATTACHING BINDING

Attach the binding to your quilt using a walking foot. (This prevents puckering when sewing through the five layers.)

Choose starting point along one side of the quilt. Do not start at a corner. Match the two raw edges of the binding strip to the raw edge of the quilt top. Stitch. The pressed binding edge will be free and to left of seam line (**Photo C**). Leave a 12" or longer tail of binding strip dangling from beginning point.

Learn binding!
HeyQuilty.com/Binding

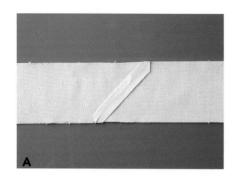

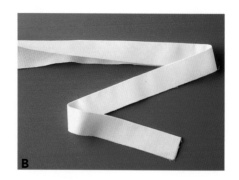

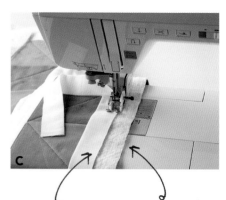

Raw edge

Batting to be trimmed off later.

SPOOLY SAYS:

"According to a 2010 survey, 73% of quilters are online. The Internet is a great tool for inspiration, instruction, and community."

(Quilting In America Survey, 2010-Creative Crafts Group.)

MITERED CORNERS

1. Place a pin ¼" from corner to mark where you will stop stitching. Stop stitching ¼" from corner; backstitch, and remove quilt from sewing machine. Rotate quilt quarter turn and fold binding straight up, away from corner, forming 45-degree-angle fold (**Photo D**). Bring binding straight down in line with next edge to be sewn, leaving top fold even with raw edge of previously sewn side (**Photo E**). Begin stitching at top edge, sewing through all layers.

2. Stop stitching about 8" away from starting point, leaving about a 12" tail at end. Bring beginning and end of binding to center of 8" opening and fold each back, leaving about ¼" space between the two folds of binding (**Photo F**). Finger press the folds. Allowing this ¼" extra space is critical, as binding tends to stretch when it is stitched to the quilt. If the folded ends meet at this point, your binding will be too long for the space after the ends are joined.

3. Open binding and draw line across wrong side of binding on fold line, as shown (**Photo G**). Draw line along lengthwise fold of binding at same spot to create an X (**Photo H**).

D

E

F

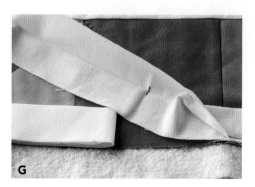

G

H

Boot Camp

4. With edge of ruler at marked X, line up 45-degree angle marking on ruler with one long side of binding (**Photo I**). Draw diagonal line across binding as shown (**Photo M**). Repeat for other end of binding. Lines must angle in same direction (**Photo J**).

5. Pin binding ends together with right sides facing, pin-matching diagonal lines as shown (**Photo K**). Binding ends will be at right angles to each other. Machine-stitch along diagonal line, removing pins as you stitch.

6. Lay binding against quilt to double check that it is correct length (**Photo L**). Trim ends of binding ¼" from diagonal seam.

7. Finger press diagonal seam open (**Photo M**). Fold binding in half and finish stitching the binding to your quilt (**Photo N**).

You're doing great!

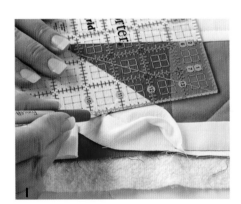

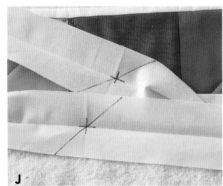

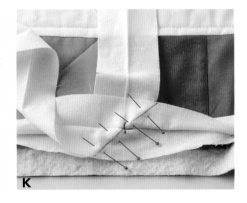

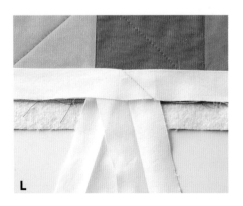

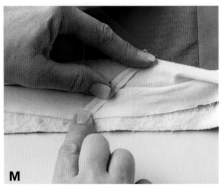

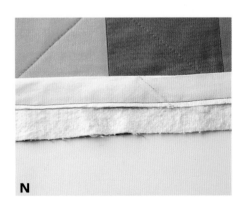

HAND STITCHING BINDING TO QUILT BACK

1. Trim any excess batting and quilt back with scissors or a rotary cutter (**Photo A**). Leave enough batting (about 1/8" beyond quilt top) to fill binding uniformly when it is turned to quilt back.

2. Bring pressed edge of binding to quilt back so that it covers machine stitching. Blindstitch folded edge to quilt backing, using a few pins just ahead of stitching to hold binding in place (**Photo B**).

3. Continue stitching to corner. Fold under unstitched binding from next side, forming a 45-degree angle and a mitered corner. Stitch mitered folds on both front and back (**Photo C**). Good job.

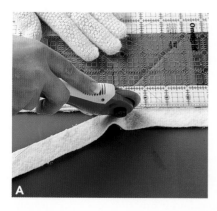 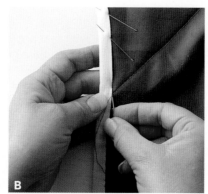 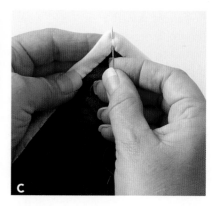

 Hungry for more video on binding? Check out Liz Porter's famous technique at: **DailyCraftTV.com/Binding**

WHY DON'T YOU...

...ask if your public library would want a quilt. Donate or make one for the wall in the children's reading room!

...make all the fabric choices for your quilt— and then reverse them.

...name your next quilt before you make it. What will "Henry" look like? Or "Spring Thaw"? Or "Vector"?

Boot Camp

Marvelous Methods
Misc. hints for making perfect blocks

As you sew more patchwork, you'll develop your own shortcuts and favorite methods. Here are a few favored by the fine folks at Quilty.

As you join patchwork units to form rows and then join your rows to form blocks, press seams in opposite directions from row to row whenever possible (Photo A). By pressing seams one direction in the first row and the opposite direction in the next row, you will create seam allowances that abut or "lock" when rows are joined (Photo B). It won't happen every time. You will end up with seam allowances facing the same direction as you join units from time to time.

If you hate it when thread bunches up at your machine's throat plate, make a spider! A spider is a small, folded fabric square that you sew on and off of when you begin or end a series of patchwork (Photo C). This gives your machine something to "chew" so it's less likely your thread will clog or get tangled. (BTW: Repeated use of the small piece of fabric gives it lots of thread "legs," which is where it gets its name.)

Trim off those tiny triangle tips or "dog ears" that happen when you make triangle-square units (Photo D). Trimming triangles greatly reduces bulk and makes patchwork units and blocks lie flat (Photo E). You want that. A smooth, flat quilt top is easier to quilt, either by hand or machine.

Careful pressing will make your patchwork neat and crisp, and will help make your finished top lie flat. Ironing and pressing are two different skills. We iron shirts, pants, and big swaths of new fabric to remove wrinkles using a back and forth, smoothing motion. But we press patchwork and quilt blocks to "set" the seams we sew. We press by raising and gently lowering the iron on our work. After sewing a patchwork unit, first press the seam just as it is, closed, fresh off your machine. This embeds the stitch. After that, open the unit and press it with the seam toward the darkest fabric, being careful to not form a pleat in your seam.

Many quilters use "finger pressing" to open and flatten seams of small units before they press with an iron. To finger press, open the patchwork unit with right side of fabric facing you. Run your fingernail firmly along seam, making sure unit is fully open with no pleat. Give it a firm crease without over-stretching.

Just like overeager finger pressing, overly aggressive ironing can stretch blocks out of shape. New quilters beware! It's a common problem when you're just getting started, but you'll get better at judging your pressing technique the more patchwork you make.

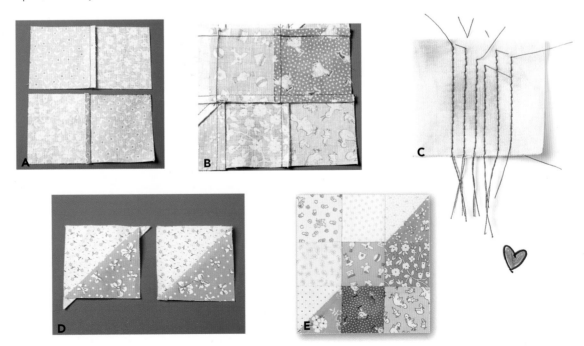